The Wisdom of the Parrot

The Wisdom of the Parrot

Chris Morley

Copyright © Chris Morley 2004

Illustrations by Fran Flannery

British Library Cataloguing in Publication data
A catalogue record for this book is available
from the British Library

ISBN 1 85852 265 X

First published by Inspire
4 John Wesley Road
Werrington
Peterborough PE4 6ZP

Printed and bound in Great Britain by
Stanley L Hunt (Printers) Ltd, Rushden, Northants

Preface

During the First World War, trained parrots were perched on the Eiffel Tower, from where they could give 20 minutes' warning of incoming aircraft. The practice was abandoned when it was discovered that the birds could not discriminate between German and Allied planes. The parrots' failure to distinguish between the planes revealed a wisdom not shown by the warring human beings.

The parrots couldn't see the difference between friend and enemy. Any wisdom found in this book starts from the assumption that another common distinction can be helpfully ignored. It's between an outer world, sometimes humdrum but often fascinating and even bizarre, and an inner world where we experience, among other emotions, love, pain, generosity, loneliness, forgiveness and a sense of mystery.

This book brings together the two areas of experience. Readers are offered a picture of some unusual human activity or natural phenomenon which becomes a way into a deepened awareness of comfort, challenge or excitement at the spiritual level. The thoughts encourage the imagination to roam freely around the images offered and find in them nourishment for the heart.

Christianity is at its heart a faith in which the material world is a vehicle for spiritual truth.

This book sees the two as one. That's how the parrots viewed the planes. Perhaps there'll be something to learn from 'the wisdom of the parrot'.

Contents

A deeper beauty

Valerie Lord has developed a new version of the Japanese Haiku. Instead of that tradition's 17-syllable poems, she has produced one of 15 words:

Clouds graze the sky

below sheep drift gentle over fields

soft mirrors warm white snow

The additional novelty is that the poem is written one word on the back of each of 15 sheep. You could call it a Haik-ewe.

The point of this interesting way of presenting poetry, which, the poet was at pains to make clear, caused the sheep no pain, is that the words then become fluid. As the sheep move around the field, they form different patterns creating different meanings. She has, in a sense, relinquished control of the poetry – it is the sheep who now create its form. They are presumably unaware that they are part of an artistic project so the beauty and meaning that still occasionally emerge do so in an entirely random way.

Our lives consist of continually changing patterns made up of their various components. Often we feel more comfortable if we are in control of the pattern, of how the different parts of our lives fit together and in what order things happen. Sometimes, however, things happen that feel entirely random but which create new meaning and beauty. They may have been something God intended to happen but they were not part of any plan of ours.

Let's be less determined to control today's events. It may be that, if we relinquish control, interesting and apparently random occurrences may add a new depth to our lives.

A friend of ours owns six Siamese cats. They can be quite noisy. But they have learnt that when the phone rings, there is no use demanding attention because their owner will be otherwise occupied for a while. They have also learnt the significance of various phrases that indicate the coming to an end of the call and these inevitably lead to the starting up of the noise again. Unwilling to be defeated, Linda has discovered that she can gain some quiet to read the paper or get some p & q, simply by holding the phone to her ear.

As we go through each day, there are a number of responses we make out of habit. It would exhaust us if we could not, for part of the time, rely on our reflex-actions and let our behaviour be guided by routine rather than thought. The danger is that, just as the cats are fooled by our friend's deception, so our conditioned responses to those we live with, or to routine situations at work, can become inappropriate and empty.

When God told Abraham, at the age of 75, to leave Haran and set out for a new home (Genesis 12.1-4), this was but the first of many times in the Bible when God urged a break from routine. Often the challenge was resisted but the change God offered was always for the better.

Perhaps today we could achieve a deeper beauty by being open to new possibilities in our lives and checking occasionally to make sure that, if any of our behaviour is automatic, the habit is one we feel happy with.

Roughly the size of a pendant, the Verbatim Store n' Go can be hung round the neck, a new type of fashion statement. It's for people for whom the number of computer files they need to carry around with them can no longer be accommodated by an ordinary diskette. This drive can store up to 1 gigabyte and so you could choose to wear it, if you wished, to ensure that you'll be recognised, by those in the know at least, as very important and very busy.

Many of us, even if more subtly, like to carry around with us an aura of busy-ness. Jesus described (Matthew 23.27) people who did this in his day as like 'whitewashed tombs', graves which look beautiful on the outside but contain only death. Strong language – he was obviously angered by this human characteristic – and the truth of the matter is that none of us are actually dead inside. But the warning is there – that wanting to give others a particular impression of ourselves can eat away at our true life.

Perhaps today we could concentrate on rediscovering that life. What we feel passionate about and committed to, what delights us and nourishes us, what motivates and inspires us – these are the things that make us who we are. When we are in touch with them and feel really alive, any remaining need to advertise our importance will disappear. We won't end up wearing a computer drive round our necks; though, probably without trying to, we may find we're wearing our hearts on our sleeves.

Searched and known

There's a new Dyson vacuum cleaner on the market. When it breaks down, the mechanic will connect a microchip inside it to a phone. This will send all necessary information about the machine's history and performance to the call centre so that the cause of the fault can be easily discovered and put right.

Human problems cannot be sorted out so easily. If something goes wrong with our lives, we struggle to understand, let alone repair, our failings and shortcomings. No human being knows us well enough to suggest a completely reliable remedy.

The Psalmist suggests, however, that God may have that insight. 'You have searched me and known me … You are acquainted with all my ways … It was you who formed my inward parts'(Psalm 139). Christians believe that God knows us well enough to help us deal with those things that go wrong and prevent us from living up to our potential. Our relationship with God is not mechanical and the process of change is normally slow; but it is encouraging to know there is someone who understands and can help us.

Sometimes other people know us so well that we are grateful for their wisdom and advice. God knows us fully. It's not quite so simple as putting a phone and a microchip together but it's good to know there's someone whose forgiving and healing love can be trusted to help put us right.

When *Top of the Pops* began to suffer from flagging viewing figures, its producers reinvented it. It became the *All New Top of the Pops* with fewer songs, more interviews and news, new logo, new theme tune, new everything – and famous people to launch the new format. These included Posh Beckham, who chose the occasion to relaunch her solo career by singing both sides of her new single, one pop and the other hip-hop, and asking the audience to vote on which they preferred. This would guide her, we were told, in deciding which of the two types of music to focus on for her next release. 'Change as much as possible' seemed to be the watchword for *All New Top of the Pops*; letting other people decide your future direction was the gimmick favoured by Victoria Beckham's record company.

There are times when the idea of relaunching our lives might appeal. Lack of success, unhappiness, struggling with a relationship, feeling envious of other people's lives, might all be motives for wanting a fresh start. But it isn't normally possible to stop and start again. Jesus told a story (Luke 15.11-32) about a son who asked his father for a share of the inheritance he was due later, so that he could relaunch his life somewhere else. It didn't work. The real new beginning came when he came back to his father and found that he was loved and accepted for who he was in spite of the money he had wasted.

Making as many changes in life as possible, or trying to fit in more with other people's expectations, won't in the end make much difference. Let's be grateful today for anybody who loves and accepts us even though we continue to be frustrated; it is that kind of accepting love which will begin to relieve the frustration and enable us to discover a greater contentment with who and where we are.

A Singapore company has a high-tech solution for absent-minded drivers who lose their cars in multi-storey car parks. Forgetful drivers, stressed by what they've been doing since they parked their car, key in their licence plate number at a kiosk. A map appears on a screen indicating the zone and space where the car is parked. Similar devices positioned around our homes might be useful in saving time spent looking for things we 'know we put somewhere'.

It isn't only our possessions that get lost, though. Bits of ourselves sometimes get hidden out of sight. A woman once crept up behind Jesus to touch what he was wearing. She wanted both to be healed and to avoid a scene (Mark 5.24-34). His response, calling attention to her but with loving approval of what she had done, not only healed her but also enabled her to rediscover her lost self-confidence.

Other things that might get lost temporarily are our sense of humour, our ability to trust, our capacity for fun. Perhaps today we might check whether we have lost bits of ourselves in all the stress of our daily lives. Just to realise it may be enough to help us rediscover them. But if we would like help making good use of every part of our personalities, we can ask God, because the way Jesus behaved suggests this is something God delights to do.

We're not alone

Concorde's last flight was fully booked months before take-off, but auctions in Paris and London not long after gave ordinary punters a chance to be in on the act. Perhaps they felt that taking home a couple of front landing wheels might be an acceptable consolation prize, though the nose cone, which went for £320,000 might have been a bit beyond most of the plane's fans.

The several thousand bits and pieces from Concorde in the auctions had little real value of their own. But they were worth large amounts of money because they were part of something bigger, something majestic and beautiful.

Each human being has his or her own importance. Each one has an inestimable worth. Yet for people, too, there is an added value from being part of something big. The institutions in which they work, their wider family, the charity they support or the political campaign they are involved in, can all provide a deeper meaning to life and an enhanced sense of personal value.

For any believer in God, there is a deeper awareness of being involved in more than just what is immediately apparent. Each person who tries to be in touch with God's purposes for them expects to be a factor, perhaps without knowing it, in the working out of God's wishes for communities and even for the world as a whole.

Let's celebrate today the feeling that we are contributing to something bigger than ourselves and be grateful for the added value it gives to our lives.

What would lead anyone to swallow 95 worms in 30 seconds? Or 982 friends to want to get together to become the largest number ever to sit on whoopee cushions at the same time? Whatever it is, 60,000 such record attempts are reported each year to the *Guinness Book of Records*.

We wouldn't all do such extraordinary things to achieve recognition but we all want it, particularly if we feel we've done something especially loving or skilful, or surmounted exceptional difficulties. It's unnerving if it seems we are the only ones to have noticed how well we've done.

One of the advantages of the belief that human beings are never out of God's 'sight' is that God, if no one else, will be aware of such achievements and delight in them. It's easy to focus on the knowledge that God is aware of our failures but, on the other hand, our successes give God pleasure.

Let's today be aware of this basic human need for recognition and tell people if we notice something they've done well. If our own achievements and struggles go unacknowledged, perhaps there are ways, less ostentatious than the ones recorded in the *Guinness Book of Records*, of gently drawing them to the attention of those around us.

In the carriage GNER has designated as 'quiet' (no mobiles etc.), a man is talking to his girlfriend on the phone. A disagreement appears to be developing until finally, 'I am not shouting,' he shouts down the phone.

Our human ability to deceive ourselves is considerable. We often don't know what we are doing. We don't see ourselves as others do. Everybody else in the coach could hear what was happening. We could have told him how he was coming over to his girlfriend.

One of the purposes of prayer is to help us see ourselves as we really are. To imagine God looking at us, and asking ourselves what God sees, is a very helpful way of getting a better picture of who we are and how we might come across to others.

Sometimes also we do ourselves a favour by letting others tell us how they see us. We don't have to ask them straight out. There are more subtle ways of doing it. But perhaps today might be a day for checking out whether there is any aspect of our personalities or behaviour about which we are deceiving ourselves.

Dreaming a different future

The doctor and astrologer Nostradamus was born just over 500 years ago. He became extremely wealthy by foretelling the future to members of the French court. According to one tradition, he discovered this ability when he informed a neighbour that he would see two blackbirds on his way home. 'Well,' reported the neighbour afterwards, 'I am not sure how many there were but it was certainly black.' From this unpromising beginning emerged 6,300 predictions taking the world up to 3797 and including, supporters claim, prophesies of the rise of Hitler, the assassination of Kennedy and the death of Princess Diana.

People today also want the security of knowing what the future will bring. Some read their stars because they feel that if they know what is going to happen, or if they are able to prepare themselves for crises that might emerge, they will feel more secure.

The coming of Jesus was seen as the fulfilment of prophecy. But he offers a different kind of security. Those who believe in him feel safe, not because he tells us what will happen, but because his life and death are a commitment from God to be with us whatever the future holds.

In any worries we may have today about the future, knowing there are people around us who will support us through whatever happens is more important than knowing what might happen. Nostradamus made his money by telling French royalty their future, but God's presence with us, and the backing of our friends, is a more reliable form of security.

Carnforth railway station has become a Mecca for *Brief Encounter* fans. The buffet, where the encounter between the Celia Johnson and Trevor Howard characters began, has been restored. To go there now, you feel you are walking into the film. It's a monument to the kind of unrequited longing that the two lovers' chaste and impossible affair epitomises. The passion the pair felt for each other was intense but it was in the final scene in the buffet that it became clear it could not be fulfilled. Even so, I suspect that even without the ending they wanted, the relationship was something they would not have missed.

The popularity of the film reflects the familiarity of that experience, not just in the context of sexual attraction, but in many areas of life. We long passionately for something to happen, perhaps even work hard towards that end. It doesn't work out the way we wanted. Sometimes a different but unexpectedly satisfying outcome surprises us. But even if not, the longing, though unfulfilled, has its own value.

The biblical prophets speak of a longing for a more just and peaceful world. They express the deep yearning we all feel for an end to human violence and self-destructive behaviour. The birth of a child in a stable was not the outcome the prophets expected. Because this child was special, his coming added new power to the hope. But it hasn't, not to the human eye anyway, brought the fulfilment any nearer.

Today, even if our dreams for ourselves and our world seem far from becoming reality, let's give ourselves with renewed energy to working towards them. There may be a different outcome from the one we expect and the process, even without the fulfilment, might have a value all its own.

'Aoccdrnig to rseearch at an Elingsh uinervtisy, it deosn't mttaer in waht oredr the ltteers in a wrod are, the olny iprmoatnt tihng is taht the frist and lsat ltteer is at the rghit pclae. The rset can be a toatl mses and you can sitll raed it wouthit a porbelm. Tihs is bcuseae we do not raed ervey lteter by it slef but the wrod as a wlohe.' This is the gist of some recent research. 'As long as you can anticipate what the next word in a sentence could be, you will not necessarily notice if some of the letters in that word are out of place,' says a lecturer in neuro-psychology.

It's true in life, too, that meaning is provided by expectation. Most of the time we think we know what will happen next and, generally, life feels more comfortable if we are right. Even if the details are slightly different from what we expected, we feel we know where we are if things follow a more or less predictable course.

But when we apply this principle to our relationships, our desire for the comfort of the familiar can have an unwanted affect. If we are close to someone, our expectation of how they will behave can have a sufficiently strong impact on them to encourage precisely the predicted behaviour. So if we expect someone, for example, to be incompetent, unco-operative, humourless, they often will be. These assumptions may be based on experience but to revise them, so as to have more hopeful expectations, can help them change.

Let's today hope for the best in the people around us and be delighted when they conofnud our eptaxetcoins.

Divine presence

Not long ago, Oprah Winfrey bought a work table for $220,000. Such is the fashion for 'Shaker style' furniture in US showbiz circles. The Shakers were an eighteenth-century religious group and their furniture-making exemplified the simplicity, functionality and high quality of workmanship associated with their Quaker origins. Above all, they believed their craftsmanship was guided by divine inspiration. As the Roman Catholic monk and spiritual writer, Thomas Merton, put it: 'The peculiar grace of a Shaker chair is due to the maker's belief that an angel might come and sit on it.'

Quaint though such a thought might seem, the image can be an inspiration. Whatever kind of workmanship we are engaged in today, the idea that an angel might be a recipient of it could be an added incentive to give of our best.

In 2003, the winner of the Plain English Campaign's 'Foot in Mouth' award for the most baffling statement by a public figure was US Defence Secretary Donald Rumsfeld. 'Reports that say that something hasn't happened are always interesting to me because, as we know, there are known knowns, there are things we know we know,' Rumsfeld said, 'We also know there are known unknowns; that is to say we know there are some things we do not know. But there are also unknown unknowns – the ones we don't know we don't know.' 'We think we know what he means,' said Plain English Campaign spokesman John Lister. 'But we don't know if we really know.'

Donald Rumsfeld is not the only one who sometimes finds it tricky saying just what he means. Even when what we are trying to say is comparatively straightforward, we can become tongue-tied. But, as Mr Rumsfeld was probably saying, conveying something that is complicated, or where we don't know the full story or where there is an element of mystery, can become almost impossible to do in words.

St John describes the birth of Jesus as the Word becoming flesh. The mystery of God's love for the human race, and why God persists with it in spite of rejection after rejection, is one of the things we know we don't know. There is also much about God that we don't yet know we don't know. But St John believed that as human beings open themselves to the birth, life and death of Jesus, an understanding develops that is deeper and truer than words can convey.

We will never be able fully to comprehend life's mystery but perhaps in the Word come down to earth there are answers that are beyond the ability of language to express.

A best-selling book by Lynne Truss is called *Eats, Shoots and Leaves*. It's about punctuation and the title is based on a joke. An irate panda walks into a café, orders a sandwich, eats it, draws a gun and fires two shots into the air. When he's gone the waiter finds a badly punctuated wildlife manual open at a page which described what happened: Panda. Large black-and-white bear-like mammal, native to China. Eats, shoots and leaves.

Too much punctuation can create completely the wrong meaning. Not enough can make a sentence sound meaningless. Punctuation indicates the length of the pause between the words and the right amount of silence is required to give the intended meaning.

Many people consider God to be too silent. They would prefer more guidance and more words of comfort for themselves; and more instruction and, perhaps, more condemnation for others. Part of the process of trusting God is accepting that God discloses to human beings exactly what is appropriate. It may not always feel like it but God reveals as much as we need to know to find meaning for our lives.

The amount of silence in God's communication is the amount required to enable us most accurately to discern what God wants to say.

Such discernment grows with experience of trying to listen to God. The ability to know when to speak and when to be silent in our relationships with other people is also a skill it takes time and attentiveness to develop. Perhaps we might continue that learning process today and be particularly aware of those moments when silence is more appropriate than speaking.

Down-to-earth

The Djenne Mosque in Mali is built of mud and every year 40,000 people gather to repair the damage caused to its walls by the rainy season. They use the trunks of palm trees which are left sticking out of the walls to clamber up and restore the smoothness and strength of the exterior. The building is created out of one basic element, the earth, and is vulnerable to the power of another, the weather. It is kept in good repair by people who depend on nature and their own hard labour for their survival.

Christians believe that God chose to be part of earthly life, to become as dependent on its elemental forces as every other human being. You couldn't get much closer to the soil than being born in a stable. Christ seems to have delighted in the natural world. He represented God's involvement in the most basic aspects of human living and of God's sharing in the basic human struggle to survive.

In the West, we are not so in touch with nature as in other parts of the world. But today we can enjoy the feel of the weather on our skin and the contact of our hands with material things. We, like those who annually repair the mosque, can find spiritual nourishment in being close to the physical world.

The clutter that a modern copper carries is a far cry from the days when the bobby on the beat had to rush to the nearest police phone box to summon help. But it was like that in 1963 when the *Dr Who* series first began. It was just such a police phone box which became the time-travelling Tardis used by the Doctor when he needed to disappear from the dangers of the present to some hopefully safer future or past.

We too might wish we were somewhere else. In our case it might be because we're bored, afraid, frustrated or embarrassed. But we know that if we could escape we would, in the long run, be worse off. It is often through such situations that we are offered opportunities to grow and mature.

The desire to escape was one Jesus knew. His prayer in the Garden of Gethsemane was that he might not have to face the death that confronted him. But face it he did, and his courage and eventual emergence from the grip of death demonstrates the power that can come from staying with painful situations.

Perhaps today if we feel like running away, we might ask ourselves instead what we could learn, about ourselves or about life, by staying and dealing with whatever the situation is. It might also be that in facing such situations, we discover that God makes a point of becoming known to us precisely in those places and experiences which we would not have chosen.

23

Every summer, when they are not so busy, Father Christmases from as far afield as Japan and El Salvador gather in Copenhagen for the three-day annual World Santa Claus Congress. I wonder what they talk about: what reindeers like to eat, or the look on the faces of children when they receive a gift and the pleasure it gives to be the donor? Will they share together a pride in representing a character whom the myth regards as totally devoted to giving to others, without any expectation of return?

It's sometimes said that when children discard their belief in Father Christmas, their belief in that other man in the sky with the long beard goes with it. Indeed, if that is how they have been brought up to think of God, it's a good thing too.

But let's hope they don't decide that people who give to others without expecting anything back also only exist in a world of fantasy. That's what God is like. It's what Christian people, and people of other faiths and beliefs, are like, at their best. We want children's experience, not just of Christmas, but of life, to include real and frequent experience of such generosity.

Today, let's share with others our love and our possessions, without expecting anything in return – in doing so, we are enabling each other, and not just children, to experience God, a God who, far from being up in the clouds, is very much down-to-earth.

The voice within

An inmate in an American prison wrote to seek advice from a computer magazine: Eye strike a key and type a word and weight four it two say weather eye am write oar wrong, it shows me strait a weigh. As soon as a mist ache is maid, it nose bee fore eye can put the error rite, its rare lea wrong. Eye have run this poem threw it, so am shore your pleased two no its letter perfect awl the weigh – my chequer tolled me sew.

The questioner wanted a fail-safe spell-checker but, of course, there isn't one. Only he knows what he actually wants to say and, as with the rest of life, it's not appropriate to let someone else make our decisions for us. Christians will want to include God in the decision-making process, using prayer as a way of letting God offer guidance and prompting. Most people have friends or family with whom they will wish to talk over any major development in their lives. But in the end it is important that each person makes up their own mind in matters that affect them.

Let's today be grateful for those we can ask to prompt us as we try to get things right in our lives and be proud of decisions we have made which turned out well.

In May 1953, Edmund Hillary and Tenzing Norgay reached the top of Everest. They had had their sights on this achievement for years and it's hard to imagine their sense of triumph when, finally, they stood on the summit. Strange how different people can be. I'm happy with a stroll up a Welsh hill and feel not at all inadequate because of my more limited ambition. Indeed, if I were to join one of the guided tours you can now take to Everest's summit, inspiring though the prospect of the view from the top might be, I am sure I would never get there.

It is very important that our goals in life are the right ones for us. It's so easy to adopt other people's aims for our lives, or to feel somehow inferior because our aims in life are simple. St Paul, writing to Christians at Rome (Romans 12.3), tells them to think their way to a 'sober judgement' of their abilities and strengths. To overreach ourselves is to set ourselves up for failure. To put ourselves down is to opt to stay in the foothills. The summits on which we set our sights need to be ones we have chosen because that is where we want to be, and where we could be.

There's an annual convention at the National Exhibition Centre for keepers of caged birds. The hall is full of proud owners displaying their pets, many of which speak volubly. In fact so loud is the noise of parrots and budgerigars that mere humans can hardly hear what their companions are saying.

On one occasion, the prophet Elijah desperately needed to receive God's encouragement and guidance. He found it, not in wind, earthquake or fire, but in a gentle murmuring sound. He could so easily have missed it.

Our lives are often so fast-moving and busy that wind, earthquake and fire are suitable images for them. Our minds are often full of noise, thoughts clamouring for attention, so that it is really hard to focus on what really matters.

Perhaps today, it might be worth spending a moment pushing these surface noises aside and trying to focus on the voices that come from deeper within us.

Free to be me

Carol Aston keeps a coffin in her spare room and every so often will add something to the intricate design that adorns it. Although only 50, she's already thinking about her wish for her casket to say something, as it disappears behind the curtains or into the ground, about the kind of person she has been. Not so idiosyncratic as it sounds – she makes a living out of doing the same for other people, each one painted to order.

Does she stand any chance of getting a commission from you? Do you fancy making a 'statement' to those attending your funeral? Would it be a confident assertion of your personality and characteristics? Some of us will feel comfortable with this idea because in life, too, we have been extroverts, happy to share what's inside us and to express freely the richness of our personalities.

Or does the very idea make you cringe with embarrassment? Are you much more private, preferring not to have the limelight even at your funeral if you could help it, and keeping yourself to yourself? Perhaps you would prefer the epitaph found on an anonymous grave in Vermont:

> I was somebody. Who, is no business of yours.

Whichever kind of person we are, what is important is that we are proud of that. We each express ourselves differently and give delight to those close to us in a unique way. We are all 'somebody'. We don't need to wait for our funerals – we could valuably take time today to celebrate who we are, with others if that's our way, or perhaps just quietly on our own.

In the final scene of the 1967 film *The Graduate*, Benjamin and Elaine are finally together, escaping on a bus. Ben has rescued Elaine from a wedding in which she had been an unhappy bride. The awkwardness of the moment is brilliantly conveyed and its effectiveness is partly due to the fact that the cameras continue rolling when the actors expect them to stop. Suddenly they are no longer pretending to be uncomfortable for the sake of the plot. They really don't know where to put themselves.

All of us are acting part of the time. It can be inappropriate, for all sorts of good reasons, to let our real feelings show. So, too, all of us are being real part of the time. On our own or in trusted company, we can be true to ourselves. But most of us occasionally put on an act, when to be real would be more creative, open and honest. Sometimes what keeps us acting is fear of an unsympathetic reaction. But in making sure we avoid that, we remove the possibility of a thoroughly loving and supportive response to our real feelings.

This was the risk Nicodemus took when he went to see Jesus late one night. He let drop the mask of intellectual and priestly superiority and came honestly and openly asking questions and making himself vulnerable. He found that Jesus took him seriously and treated him with respect.

Let's today try and be aware when we are being real and when we're not. And if there's a chance that dropping the mask might give people an opportunity to care for us, let's take the risk.

Buskers on the London Underground now have to be licensed. Gone are the £200 fines for doing it illegally and in are rules: you must have an audition and a licence, must perform where you are told to on a rota basis, and must stop playing temporarily if a crowd forms. Many buskers are not happy.

Institutions often seem to inhibit creativity by the rules they make. Maybe we feel that our creative effectiveness is inhibited by having to operate within the framework of the institutions in which we work. And sometimes, too, it's easy to blame the institution for any frustration we feel.

Most of us need an external framework to operate at our best. Structures that clarify the focus of our work, provide safe boundaries and supportive colleagues, and require the minimum of maintenance, can set our creativity free.

The framework God provides for our lives has rules. The most important are that we should love God and love each other. The Christian experience is that this structure for our lives helps release each believer's full potential. As a well-known prayer suggests: '(God's) service is perfect freedom.'

Perhaps today we could contribute to any institution within which we work by seeking a balance between structure and freedom. We'll do this best, as with everything else, when we operate within the wider framework of God's way of doing things.

Being revealing

A friend of mine was to be a guest at a wedding and he was invited to look at the couple's wedding web site. There were links to various stores which held their present list and information about how to get to the wedding venues. But there was also information about how the couple met, where he proposed, what they enjoy about each other. My friend felt this was a little over the top. He was surprised, and rather uncomfortable, about looking at what felt too intimate for public perusal. It was all a bit voyeuristic.

Perhaps today we can celebrate our right to privacy. It is entirely our choice how much we share of what goes on inside us. We can choose who to tell about the personal details of our daily lives. We can keep what we want to ourselves; we can share with a few intimate friends or our partner; we could put it on the web for anyone who wishes to see it.

For Christians, one of those with whom we choose to share our intimate lives is God. It is sometimes said that God sees and knows everything. God may be capable of knowing everything about us but God is no voyeur. If we human beings regard respect for the other's privacy as important in any relationship, the chances are high that God will also value each person's freedom to keep parts of their lives to themselves. It is our choice, but those who do open their lives to God find a warm, understanding and loving response.

As we go through today we will be making choices all the time, mostly without really thinking about it, as to how open or private to be. Let's be grateful the decision is ours.

Each year in November the Bridge Inn in Santon Bridge, Cumbria, holds the Biggest Liar in the World Competition. There is a small prize and a coveted title for the lie that most impresses the panel of judges. It all goes back to the nineteenth century when the publican Will Ritson used to delight locals with his talent for bending the truth.

There are times when it is appropriate to bend the truth. Being entirely honest is not always the most loving thing to do. Telling people things it won't benefit them to know but which may cause them pain is usually unnecessary. Sometimes it is best to wait for the right moment before passing on information.

All that, however, is very different from deliberate lying. 'Bearing false witness against a neighbour', the kind of lying which deliberately hurts other people or their reputations, is one of the things forbidden in the Ten Commandments. Then there's the kind of lie which we use simply to get ourselves out of a fix or because it makes life easier for us than speaking the truth.

As today we have to make decisions about whether to tell the truth, to bend it or to lie, let's make sure that in any situation where we feel it's right to be less than truthful, it is because it is more loving to do so.

Office flirtation on the phone is apparently quite common. A routine business phone call can, if the voice and manner are mutually appealing, lead to further conversations of an increasingly intimate kind. Of course, these conversations don't reveal, unless by choice, important facts like age and physical appearance, and it's apparently easier to keep other details to yourself as well. The author of the magazine article in which I read about this suggested that this was the attraction of such flirtation. It is much easier not to be quite truthful than when meeting in person. But if you decide that you want it to become serious, the real test is whether you can trust the other person with the truth.

Most of us censor what we let others see of ourselves. It's risky revealing too much of ourselves – we choose to whom we do it because some will judge us and find us wanting. But to be truthful about ourselves and to be accepted is wonderful.

Jesus once had a conversation (John 4.4-30) with a woman who felt the need to hide from him her current living arrangements with a man to whom she was not married and her unsuccessful, and probably painful, earlier marital arrangements. But Jesus saw through this and when she realised he was still happy to spend time with her, she blossomed.

We could make someone else's day by being the kind of accepting, generous person with whom they feel they can be truthful about themselves. We might also find that in return we get a chance to be open about ourselves too.

Letting be

When it was decided to fill the fourth and empty plinth in Trafalgar Square, Londoners were asked to choose between six possible sculptures. Among other proposals were what looked like a skyscraper made of Meccano, a car which pigeons had adorned, and pieces which continued the Square's tradition as a place to celebrate victory or to protest. Voting was invited via a web site but many indicated they did not find any of the offered possibilities inspiring. For each sculpture, there were at least as many critics as admirers.

A seventh possibility, which was not in the running, was to leave it empty, with an invitation to passers-by to use their own imagination to fill the space. This idea had the merit of encouraging those who stand and view the plinth not to find fault with the work of others but to engage in some visual creativity of their own.

Jesus commented on how people want to remove a speck of sawdust from another's eye but don't even notice the plank in their own (Matthew 7.3-5). It is much easier to see other people's faults and very tempting to mention them. It's sometimes useful to take time before doing so, to ask ourselves if we, in their situation, would be doing any better. Or to wonder what blemishes they might have noticed in our lives.

We might have fun today imagining what we'd have put on the empty plinth. Or we could instead try putting one of the people we often want to criticise on a pedestal. Noticing their good qualities will be more conducive to our inner well-being than finding fault.

Scrabble players worldwide were outraged when it was suggested that mobile phone-style text slang may become acceptable in this popular word game. Shortened words like 'luv' and acronyms like PCM (please call me) and CU NXT WK might be included, said the game's makers, but the Association of British Scrabble Players was vehemently opposed to the change. It didn't honour the purity of the English language.

Texting is the new way of communicating. Over 58 million texts are sent each day in the UK. But many, especially of an older generation, simply don't like its technological complications and the slang abbreviations that are often used. Some contemporaries of Jesus did not like his style. They felt that his way of teaching about God did not do justice to God's purity and holiness. His origins too – birth in a stable of poor parents – did not seem to justify his claim to be speaking on God's behalf. A criminal's death on a cross seemed to some to be the final evidence that this man could not be God's new way of communicating with human beings.

Nothing is good simply because it's new. But sometimes our resistance to change inhibits the discovery of new things which will improve our lives. Let's today be open to what's new and hope to find it enriching.

The 28,000-strong Left-Handers Club organises an annual Left-Handers Day. The 87 per cent of the nation who are right-handed will be encouraged to experiment by using their left hands to operate ticket barriers and scissors, to try eating in restaurants without bumping elbows or writing with ink without smudging what they've just written.

The value of days like this is that they broaden awareness of the effects of such disadvantages. There are many other such ways in which people find life harder to cope with because of physical difference or appearance, or because of social or economic status.

Jesus picked out such people to be with. Widows, prostitutes, tax-collectors were often his chosen companions. Not, it seems, because he wanted particularly to help them or because they needed special support and encouragement. The impression we get from the accounts of his life was that he just liked their company. As if living outside the mainstream, in one respect or another, gave them a more interesting, perhaps a more rounded, outlook on life.

Most of us have something which makes us different from the majority of those around us. If there's nothing outwardly obvious, then something about our experience of life or what we believe can make us feel set apart from others. It might be worth asking ourselves what effect this difference has had on our lives and our outlook. Left-handed players of racquet sports have a distinct advantage when playing a right-hander. Perhaps there are ways in which our experience of being out of the ordinary has given us a valuable and alternative way of looking at life.

Growing pains

The Maglev train can reach 360 miles an hour on an experimental track west of Tokyo. It is gradually being brought into commercial use. The secret of its speed is that it doesn't touch the track. Magnetic force enables the train to float just above it as it travels, thus eliminating friction.

A life without friction sounds appealing. Not to be slowed down by other people's resistance to our wishes, or by circumstances which get in the way of what we want to achieve, sounds as though it has a lot to commend it. But friction and a slower pace can have their advantages. Encountering opposition provides opportunity for redefinition or redirection of established goals. Sometimes it is in the interaction between our selves and others or in response to new circumstances that we discover our aims more clearly and grow as people.

It appears God recognises the value of friction. There are various explanations of why the world does not automatically go the way God wants it to, but it certainly doesn't. Human beings are constantly standing in the way of God's purposes. But God chooses to work with this resistance, refines the way forward to take account of it and is constantly creating imaginative ways of moving us forward positively in spite of it.

Perhaps today, if there are moments of frustration, we might try looking for ways of turning it to our advantage by asking what we might learn from the experience of feeling hindered by people or circumstances.

While Nelson Mandela was incarcerated on Robben Island, he painted. Barbed wire, a watchtower, the indoor tennis court were all subjects he drew. So was the hospital. 'I remember the stark hospital wards with fondness,' wrote the artist in some notes about the pictures. 'These memories, like this sketch, are filled with joyous colours.' He describes the hospital as a vital link with the rest of the world, where news trickled through to inmates.

It was in the place where inmates were taken when they were at their weakest that they received strength from beyond the prison walls. St Paul, too, says that in his experience, it is when he is weak that he is strong (2 Corinthians 12.10). Many people discover unexpected reserves of strength when they are up against it. Sometimes these come from outside, and many Christians vouch for the support of Christ's energy in these situations. Sometimes it is inner resources that are revealed by the need to cope with a crisis.

Let's today rejoice in the mystery of the human capacity to find strength even, and perhaps especially, in times of weakness. Perhaps in our own lives, we can recall such occasions and, whether we are aware of the source of the strength or not, be grateful for it.

El Totumo, in Atlántico in Colombia, is one of the world's largest mud volcanoes. It was created by natural gases emitted by decaying organic matter underground. The mud is pushed upwards by the gas and it hardens above ground. As more mud oozes out and spills over the edge, it grows in size, and El Totumo is 15 metres high. At the top is a rich, creamy mud crater in which visitors are encouraged to bathe. The mud's qualities are indisputably good for the skin.

The mud becomes available because it is surfaced for us by gas from dead, decaying and disintegrating material. In our lives, too, what seems just useless waste can also sometimes have a value. Times of failure and pain seem to have no purpose. Yet these experiences, recycled mysteriously within us, often become the source of creative and positive changes in our personalities and ways of being. They can purify and refresh, and lead to wiser decisions and deeper understanding of ourselves and others.

Christian belief in Christ's death and resurrection represents this same process. Christ's new life was stronger because it had emerged from the decay of death.

If today we are experiencing pain and failure which just seem wasteful, let's not dismiss these experiences but allow our psyches to process them. We might become stronger people as a result.

Seizing the moment

Dolphins at the Marine Mammal Institute, Mississippi, are trained to help keep the pools clean. They will be rewarded with a fish if they bring a piece of litter to a trainer. Kelly has taken this task one step further. She hides litter she finds under a rock at the bottom of the pool. The next time a trainer passes she goes down to the rock and tears off a piece of paper to give to the trainer. After a fish reward, she goes back down, tears off another piece of paper, gets another fish, and so on.

Kelly has worked out how to maximise the potential in a situation. She is intelligent enough to exploit to her best advantage the possibilities the trainers' bright idea offers her.

In one of his stories (Luke 16.1-8), Jesus praises the quality of shrewdness. An estate manager was given the sack and, in order to gain some allies for the hard, unemployed times which lay ahead, he reduced the sum owed by two of his master's debtors by the amount of his own commission. His master congratulated him on his astuteness.

The ability to see the possibilities in every situation and to act with boldness and cunning to achieve them is a valuable Christian as well as human quality. Let's enjoy today the challenge of making the most of the situations we are in.

A door at our local Leisure Centre says on it:

Careful

Glass

Personally I find that reassuring. Some glass isn't. If you happen to be looking at what's beyond the glass instead of at what's right in front of you, you can end up with quite a bruise. Of course, it's always the glass's fault!

Looking to the future instead of being attentive to what's happening now can also have unwanted consequences. We can miss opportunities for new developments in our lives, and possibilities for fun and enjoyment, by keeping our attention focused only on what lies ahead. They are often there right in front of our eyes if we did but look for them.

We have no one but ourselves to blame for this. God often carefully puts such delights right in our paths. But if our minds are too much on the future, they won't come up and hit us. Once missed, they are often missed for ever.

Perhaps today we might keep our eyes open for what's staring us in the face.

Eating an orange —
savour each segment individually

We will each live, if all goes well, for about 40 million minutes. Sounds a lot. But each one matters.

Jesus told a story (Luke 12.16-21) about a farmer who was always looking forward to a good life but never got the chance to enjoy it because of his obsession with building up the wealth to make the most of it. 'Live for now,' Jesus is saying, 'you don't know how long you've got.'

The Buddhist Thich Nhat Hanh was on a lecture tour in the States. 'I must,' he said to his western guide, 'teach you how to eat an orange.' 'But I have just eaten one,' replied his companion. 'I don't think you did eat it,' said Thich Nhat Hanh. 'I noticed that after you had peeled the orange, you placed one segment of it into your mouth and immediately took another segment into your hand before swallowing the first one. And when you placed the second segment in your mouth, you immediately seized a third one. All the time your mind was on the next segment. You were in such a hurry to eat the whole orange that you never actually ate a single segment of it.'

Each minute is an important segment of our lives. Today, let's relish each one of them before moving on to the next.

Making waves

Peasant farmers from Veracruz in Mexico regularly protest at slowness in the progress of their land claims by baring their bottoms. Cars honk, children smirk and most adults smile as the farmers strip off in Mexico City, stand by the roadside for a while, and get dressed again. Turning the other cheek, you might say.

The tactic for the peasants is a serious one, as it was for Jesus when he used that phrase (Matthew 5.39). In positions of powerlessness, our only weapon is sometimes that very defencelessness. When we are willing to reveal our vulnerability, we lay ourselves open to being taken advantage of. But we also put ourselves at the mercy of the people oppressing us in a way that is strong and assertive and expresses our freedom, not our enslavement.

We may today be experiencing a situation where we feel helpless in the face of abuses of power. They can occur at work, and even in families, as well as in more political contexts. Despair of ever changing the situation can sap our energy. But a strategy to draw attention to our vulnerability in an assertive way can revitalise us. We need to use our imaginations to come up with appropriate forms of words or actions, but, especially if they are funny and done in concert with others, the equivalent of turning the other cheek can be surprisingly effective.

My late mother-in-law lived under one of the Heathrow flight paths. Most days there was no problem but on the days when the flight controllers chose that path for incoming flights, it could be quite deafening. On one occasion, Kit was throwing a party in the garden and the guests could hardly hear themselves speak. So she rang Air Traffic Control. 'We're having a party under the flight path you are using today,' she said. 'Would you mind changing it to another?' And they did.

We sometimes take for granted the right of others to take decisions that affect us. But often we can, instead, just ask for what we want.

Christians see Christ's rising to life, after being put to death by the authorities of the time, as a victory over all powers that make people fearful. It is an encouragement not to be frightened of asserting our own power in order to create a richer, more humane life for us or for others.

Other people's unreasonable behaviour sometimes restricts our lives. Often it could be changed without serious effects. Perhaps today we could try asking them.

Screw-capped wine bottles can eliminate cork taint, say the experts, but *Which* magazine found that 74 per cent of consumers think such bottles are not so socially acceptable.

Ten thousand Women's Institute members were once surveyed by a tea merchant in Minehead to discover whether, for the best taste, milk should be added before or after the tea.

Yet 45 per cent of the population in the Congo have no access to clean water and 66 per cent of the world's population are facing critical water shortages in the next 25 years.

How do we respond to such painful inequality? Jesus's story (Luke 16.19-31), about a rich man and the poor man who begged at his gate, suggests an answer. When they both die, the chasm that existed between them on earth is reflected in heaven, but now it is the rich man who experiences desperate thirst. He wants Lazarus to come to his aid with some water.

The rich man never got past seeing Lazarus as a dogsbody to do his bidding. He was never a real individual. So, too, statistics can widen the chasm between the wealthy and the poor by removing the individuality of each hungry or thirsty adult or child. To narrow the chasm, we need the imagination and courage to see in each poor person a struggling, hurting human being. This will make us hurt too. But as we respond to this on-going tragedy, drowning our sorrows in a glass of wine or 'putting the kettle on' is not enough. We need to face the pain as the first step to discovering what appropriate action might come next.

Formulae for living

$$pn(j,k) = P\{XN+L, S=K/Xn, s=j\}, jE\ kn, kE\ Kn+1.$$

This is the formula produced by two Swiss academics to guide contestants who want to do well in *Who Wants To Be A Millionaire?* They emphasise that all ultimately depends on knowing the answers but the formula, together with the charts which go with it, following the principles of 'stochastic optimisation', will tell players when to use each lifeline and what the level of risk is if you are unsure of the answer. In the end, though, as they admit, if you haven't got the answer within you, no external strategy will help.

There are many guidelines available for doing well in life, some more complicated than others. Religious people, philosophers, astrologers, dieticians, life coaches, and many others all have their advice to give, much of it valuable. Such formulae are all very well but to really help, the encouragement from outside needs to be matched with inner conviction and determination.

Christ's teaching is probably the most widely followed of these models for living. An additional attraction is that the basic formula (love God, love your neighbour, love yourself) is backed up by God's offer to love us and to come and give us that inner encouragement and strength. That's what was happening in the birth of Jesus and still happens through his living Spirit.

Perhaps today it might be worth reflecting on the formulae for good living that inspire us, and seek the inner strength to put them into practice.

Previewing an England international, a commentator was asked what England needed to do to win. 'Score more goals than the other team,' he replied.

Sir Jack Hayward, owner of Wolverhampton Wanderers, interviewed about his plans for the club, was asked at the end of the conversation what his plans for himself were. 'Well, to keep breathing,' was his response.

There is something to be said for having uncomplicated goals in our lives. Wider strategies have their place and long-term objectives provide something to work towards, but these need to be balanced by simpler short-term goals. Something straightforward for each day, something that doesn't need detailed planning, can give our lives structure.

The writer of the Psalms came up with a phrase that has been a good guide for believers in God ever since. 'This is the day that the Lord has made; let us rejoice and be glad in it' (Psalm 118:24). That is one possible, simple goal. So is to keep breathing or to do our best. Perhaps today it's worth remembering that simple things are enough to give the day a purpose.

It is 150 years since Sir George Cayley became the first human being to take to the air. On the anniversary, Sir Richard Branson used a copy of that first human flying machine. This, we might think, was an act of eccentricity or publicity-seeking or both. But the reaction to Sir George's flight was much stronger. Trying to fly was not appropriate, it was said; we were made to keep our feet on the ground.

The Greek myth about Icarus, whose wings melted when he flew too near the sun, symbolises this belief that, by taking wings and flying, human beings are getting above themselves. In the Hebrew scriptures, the story of the Tower of Babel reflects a belief that God doesn't like human beings to get too uppity.

The New Testament, generally speaking, takes a different view. Our purpose is to draw on God's power and love so that the rich potential of human life is fulfilled in us. The Spirit of Jesus lifts us into the realms where that is possible. Human beings are still expected to know their place but their place is to fly high and become close to God.

Nelson Mandela said, 'We are powerful beyond measure … playing small doesn't serve the world. There's nothing enlightened about shrinking … we were born to make manifest the glory of God that is within us.' Let's today think big and aim high, for God's sake as well as ours.

Difficult feelings

Only *Dr Who* fans will know how to say the word 'Exterminate' properly. This phrase, each syllable precisely enunciated in a metallic voice, expressed the basic attitude to life of the good Doctor's main opponents, the Daleks. They considered themselves superior to all other races in the universe. Humanity and all the other species in the galaxy were permitted to live as their slaves – but that which they could not subjugate they destroyed.

It was because of the morality displayed by the Daleks that my mother would not let me watch the series. She didn't want me to pick up the idea that you just kill off anyone who gets in your way. Now that I am older, while I realise that's no way to behave, I'm also aware that feeling murderous is not that uncommon.

Jesus reminds his hearers of the commandment not to kill (Matthew 5.21-22) but goes on to tell us that it goes deeper than that. We should not even nurse anger. Being angry is only human. It is the nursing of those murderous feelings that causes trouble.

Today, if someone provokes in us the fleeting wish to 'exterminate' them, we need to find ways of dealing with that feeling immediately so that it doesn't get a chance to fester or, as it did with the Daleks, gradually become part of who we are.

Cheese is passé as a mouse's chief temptation. Research from Warwick University has suggested it's chocolate that they find really irresistible.

Many human beings would agree. To stop eating a chocolate bar without finishing it demands extreme self-discipline. Of course, I blame the ingredients – there must be something in them that makes them so addictive. But, then again, it might just be something about me and chocolate.

Christians are divided about where they locate the source of temptation. For some it's a hostile force – the devil – operating with a will of its own and externally to ourselves, deliberately attracting us towards what is wrong. Like the mice, unable to resist the chocolate in the modern mousetrap, we are lured to our own destruction. An alternative view is that it's not a separate entity but something inherent within each of us, and in human society, which tempts us to do what is not good for us or others.

But whether we want to put the blame onto something beyond us, or look inside ourselves for the sources of temptation, we need to be conscious of the kind of temptations to which we are susceptible. Whatever their source, the decision to give in to them is ours.

Chocolate, for most people, will do no real damage. Other temptations – to gossip, to be economical with the truth, to work too hard, to short-change those to whom we are committed – most of us know our favourites – can seriously hurt others or ourselves. Perhaps today we could renew our determination to deal with those temptations as effectively as the mousetrap does with the poor, unsuspecting mouse.

Could monkeys, with their random typing, produce Shakespeare, given enough time and typewriters? Theoretically, or so the mathematicians tell us. But when scientists tried a limited form of the experiment, a very human problem emerged. The monkeys preferred to play. They found a variety of alternative uses for the computers and preferred having fun together to the discipline of tapping the keyboard.

The human ability to concentrate, to focus on a task, to persevere towards a chosen goal, sometimes for years, is an extraordinary gift. It is a divine quality too. There is a strong biblical emphasis on God's purposefulness and total commitment (in God's case, to the task of caring for the world and its people). This is one of the ways in which we have been made 'in the image of God'.

Of course, we get distracted and find it hard to concentrate, which might indicate that we need to reconsider our goals and current tasks. Are they what we really want? Or are we just plain tired and need a rest? More often, probably, it is a sign that what we are doing, though appropriate, is demanding, and, like the monkeys, we would prefer to play.

If we feel a sense of purpose in our lives, let's be glad that we do. And in the smaller, more detailed tasks which will occupy today's time, let's delight in the satisfaction that comes from a piece of sustained work.

Regrets

In Japan each February, the Buddhist ceremony of Hari-Kuyo, Festival of the Broken Needles, is celebrated. Once only observed by tailors and dressmakers, today anyone who sews can participate. A special shrine is made for the needles, containing offerings of food, scissors and thimbles. A pan of tofu (soybean curd) is the centre of the shrine and all the needles that have become broken, bent and useless are inserted into it. The needles find their final resting place in the ocean as devotees wrap their tofu in paper and launch them out to sea.

Anyone who pauses to reflect on their past will be aware of things they have done and experiences they have had which no longer serve any purpose. Periods of struggle and stress, times when things went wrong, ideas and dreams that came to nothing, relationships which failed, may all be cause for regret. For better or for worse, these difficult times will have contributed to our present state of being. But either way there comes a time when it is best to put such memories out of our minds.

The people of the Old Testament celebrated the Day of Atonement by, among other things, symbolically laying on the head of a goat the rebelliousness and sin of the nation. The scapegoat was then sent off, carrying the painful memories and bitter regrets of the people into the desert.

Today it's worth asking ourselves whether there are any memories that still haunt us but no longer have any creative purpose. If so, it might be helpful to dispatch them from our minds deliberately and self-consciously. Perhaps, even though we may not be near an ocean or desert, our imaginations might come up with some symbolic way of saying goodbye to our regrets.

It was said of Bob Hope that he would go to the opening of a phone booth in a gas station in Anaheim provided they had a camera and three people there. He might even sing them his signature tune, 'Thanks for the memory'. He just loved applause. 'When I die they'd better nail the lid of the box down pretty quick – or I'll be up right away for an encore.' The number of plaudits he received for his work is reflected in the *Guinness Book of Records* where he is cited as the most honoured entertainer in the world.

Yet there was another side to his success. Although he hosted 22 Oscar ceremonies he was never awarded one himself. 'Welcome to the Academy Awards,' he said at one gala, 'or, as they are known in my house – Passover.' On his visit to the American forces in Vietnam, he was deeply puzzled when the troops showed none of the widespread enthusiasm and affection to which he was accustomed. Placards held up at his performances read 'Peace not Hope'.

All our lives contain times when we feel loved and appreciated, and when we have enough success to satisfy us. There are also times when we feel unwanted, confused about why we're being rejected, a failure in many, if not all, the areas of our lives.

If that last experience is what we are going through today, it's worth remembering that even the most apparently successful people go through times like that. Memories, even if we have to dig deep to find them, of times when we *have* felt appreciated and cared about, can help carry us through. For those memories, thanks indeed.

At Wimbledon, commentators on the tennis now have Hawk-Eye to help them interpret the play. This recent innovation provides a much wider choice of replays and opportunities for analysis, including the ability to see what, according to this new tracking technology, the player should have done.

People who are wise after the event tend to annoy us. They did not have to make the decision in the heat of the moment, so what right have they, with the luxury of not being pressured and of knowing the consequences of the decision that was made, to pontificate? Yet so often we upset ourselves in the same way, going over decisions we have made and cursing ourselves that we did not do something different.

The Christian idea of redemption is relevant here. Its meaning relies on the ancient image of purchasing the freedom of one who would otherwise have remained a slave. So the word expresses the belief that God can restore our freedom even when decisions we have made appear to us to restrict it. God redeems, and gives new potential where we feel a decision has resulted in one set of opportunities being lost. God works with us to create new possibilities. And these new possibilities start from where we are now, not where we would have been if we hadn't made that decision.

Let's not bash ourselves about the head with regrets. What's done is done, and what's important is whether, with God's help, we can find creative ways forward from where we are now.

Trusting in love

One Christmas, the National Farmers Union sent farmers CDs with tracks entitled 'dawn chorus', 'whale sounds' and 'happy turkeys'. They recommended these be played to their turkeys. 'It is well known that a stressed bird is more prone to disease,' said a spokesman. 'Most of its energy goes into being frightened rather than growing and putting on weight.'

Turkeys at Christmas time have every reason to be anxious. Even without the worry that would come from knowing what the fattening's for, unnatural ways of doing it probably cause precisely the distress which the NFU wants to alleviate.

Anxiety for humans, too, can absorb a lot of energy. Music is one way of helping ourselves to feel calmer. But we can't avoid stressful events, and, like the turkey, we all have to face the end of our lives. St Paul told the early Christians at Rome that they need have no fear. He based his assurance on the certainty that nothing could happen which would separate them from the love of God. Christ, he said, had come through the worst humanity could do and was alive to share his power with them.

Periods of tension are part of life and there is the deeper awareness of our mortality. But anxiety is often a needless waste of energy. Let's use music, or whatever works for us, to alleviate the symptoms and, at a deeper level, know that we can have complete confidence in God's love.

The Memoir Club is based in County Durham. If you seem a likely candidate, they may contact you, asking if you would like to write your autobiography. In exchange for £9,000, they'll then publish it. For the price, you get other services too, of which the most popular is the help of a ghost-writer who will spice up your life to make it more interesting reading.

Their clients must want, as I would imagine to a lesser extent do most of us, to sense that their lives have some importance beyond just the living of them. They feel that a record of what they have done will add to their significance, or at least encourage others to recognise it. There is a lack of belief that what they have done, and how they have lived, stands on its own as worthy of respect and celebration.

Jesus once referred (Luke 14.7-11) to a wedding reception where some of the guests had, uninvited, taken the most important seats. The host asked them to give way to those who had initially chosen the least important places at the table.

Most of us want recognition and respect from our families, colleagues and friends. But the way to achieve it is not to go looking. It is to live in the best way we can and trust that who we are and what we do is the best testimony to our worth.

One of the more extraordinary things about the popular *Big Brother* is that thousands of people applied to take part. Not hard to understand the lure of fame and wealth, but not so easy to see why that many people are prepared to risk the humiliation. What they hope for is to become nationally loved, but previous shows have revealed how, under the pressure of having to live with eleven strangers under the constant eye of television cameras, aspects of contestants' characters have emerged which have made them a national laughing stock or hugely unpopular.

Most people, those 10,000 perhaps excluded, feel all too conscious that there are parts of themselves that they would want nobody to see. It's under pressure that we get a glimpse of what lies within us, though most of the time we manage to keep it under control. But a glimpse is enough to make us feel that if others saw us as we really are, we too would be a laughing stock, if not worse.

Jesus seemed, on a number of occasions, to see inside the personality of the one who was speaking to him and detect 'flaws' in their character. But this never stopped him loving them. In this he revealed God's deepest characteristic, that God loves each human being no matter what they are like inside. If today we become conscious of parts of ourselves we don't like, we can be reassured that they do not stop us from being loved, at least as far as God is concerned.

Postcript

A parrot belonging to Aimee Morgana and living in New York has a vocabulary of 972 words – the same as an average three year old child. The latest word to be learnt is yoghurt. Ms Morgana has recorded the four year old African grey using 10,000 different sentences up to 15 words long. Seeing another parrot hanging upside down, for example, N'kisi is said to have called out: 'You gotta put this bird on the camera.'

The key to the parrot's success is that the usual method of training by a system of rewards has been ignored in favour of a policy of talking to the parrot as if it were a human child. Treating the bird as highly intelligent and with more respect than it really deserved has apparently helped develop its linguistic skill and confidence.

Human beings, too, thrive when they are taken seriously. We give of our best when we feel trusted and appreciated. Christians believe that God trusts in us and treats us with respect even when we least deserve it. God's confidence in us releases more of our potential than any system of reward and punishment could achieve. In our everyday relationships, too, we can encourage others by having faith in them and hope that others will do the same for us.

Many human beings have an inclination to put themselves down and to undermine the effect of God's and others' trust in them. N'kisi has had the wisdom to take on board his owner's trust in him. We too may well exceed expectation if we emulate the wisdom of this particular, remarkable parrot.